DEVOTIONS
From The Earth

Deserts

Meeting God in the Dry Places

Contents

The Six Week Reading Plan

This reading plan will allow you to do the short daily readings over a five day span, then give yourself some extra time to reflect and take a few notes on the sixth day. If you do the daily readings Monday - Friday, and then take some time to journal and reflect on Saturday, you can take a break on Sundays, as you meet with other believers. Give the Holy Spirit some space to confirm or expand on things you've read during the week in a church setting.

I recommend taking some time on Saturdays to get out into nature (even if it's just your backyard) to skim over the last five readings, talk to Papa about what He wants you to learn, and jot down some notes. Make this a time of solitude to listen and learn with your favorite blend of coffee.

The journaling pages are short, so you can keep your notes brief and to the point. It is easy to later review what you've written, and quickly be reminded of meaningful insights. But if you're someone who loves to write, you might want to do your journaling in a separate book.

Introduction

"...they looked toward the desert, and there was the glory of the Lord appearing in the cloud."
Exodus 16:10 NIV

If you've ever visited a desert place, you know the scorching sun beats down and the landscape seems barren and lifeless. We can sometimes find ourselves in a spiritual desert as well. It's easy to feel lost and alone in such a place, but it's often in these desert places that we experience God's presence in a profound and life-changing way.

They say a spiritual desert can be a place of great testing and refinement, where we are forced to rely on God in a deeper way than ever before. It can also be a place of revelation, where we can see God's hand at work, even if it is sometimes only evident in retrospect.

But as we journey through our deserts, we can find hope and strength in God's promises. Even in the middle of our trials, God is at work, helping us to let go of the old, bring in new life and build up our character.

In my childhood, I spent some years growing up in the California desert. Then more recently, I lived in the Arizona desert. I have some first hand experience of how the desert can take the physical life out of you. I've also experienced the beauty of a desert in full super bloom that takes your breath away. Every place God created has it's own kind of beauty and grace.

I share some of my life stories in this book. Some will inspire wonder in the creation, reminding us what an awesome God we serve. Other stories hit closer to the heart and remind us how to find comfort in the precious Holy Spirit, and how much we need him.

My hope is that these pages will help you take comfort in knowing that even in the driest, most desolate places, God is with you, leading you to new growth and life, and showing us the beauty that is right in front of us.

May the Lord bless you through this journey. ~Author

Week One

Red Rocks

I'll never forget it. I was starting to hike up the red rocks, and honestly, it was as if I heard the rock say, "You have the answers. You are your teacher." I thought I was having an auditory hallucination. *~Gwyneth Paltrow*

Isaiah 61:3 NIV
...to bestow on them a crown of beauty instead of ashes, the oil of joy instead of mourning, and a garment of praise instead of a spirit of despair.

The red rocks of Sedona are one of the most beautiful desert places in the world. These kind of landscapes make you wonder how they came to be. I believe the Lord gave us this amazing scenery just for the beauty of it!

When I lived in Arizona, I made many trips to Sedona. It was usually full of tourists, but the beauty of the rocks kept drawing me back. The colorful layers and towering spires always had me dropping my jaw at the beauty of the area. The wonder of this place was revealed out of the chaos of events in the far past. Beauty for ashes. That's what God does.

Time spent in nature is always great therapy, and pushes away the pressures and heaviness of life. You may not be able to visit the red rocks, but any place in nature that makes you smile and relax will do.

Sometimes, in our desert moments, it can feel like we are in a low place. But it's in those places that we can hear the voice of God speaking to us louder. Why? Because we are listening. We listen better when our lowliness presses in and all we can do is look up.

As you journey through the deserts of your life, remind yourself of his presence in all things, and get lost in the possibilities of what beauty he will bring about out of your chaos. He always has a plan, and works everything out for our good.

Thank you Father for bringing the beauty out of my ashes. Thank you for hearing me and guiding me when my spirit is in a desert place. Amen

Frozen Desert

We were marooned in a frozen desert. There was not a sign of life on the horizon and a thousand signs of death... The marvel is we did not all die of cold.
~Wilfred Owen

Psalm 29:8 NIV
The voice of the Lord shakes the desert;
the Lord shakes the Desert of Kadesh.

Deserts are usually known for their scorching heat and relentless sun, but in some regions or seasons, they can be bitterly cold as well. I remember a road trip I took as a young adult, where I saw a snow covered desert for the first time. I was in awe. Another aha moment in discovering something new about planet Earth! At that time I had no idea you could freeze in the desert. I was truly surprised.

Physical cold is one thing, but a frozen heart can take the warmth out of living. Sometimes hurtful experiences can make us grow cold toward others and life in general. It can be hard to overcome those feelings. This is where forgiveness can set us free. It may sound simplistic, but I truly believe the only way to get past deep hurts is to dig them up from the deep and bring them to our Jesus. These kind of wounds are exactly what he came to heal.

Maybe you are one of the lucky ones that has had a sweet life surrounded by love. I'm truly happy for you, and I hope you never have to feel the pain of a cold heart. Maybe you know someone who is hurting this way that you can help with this message. When we are in these cold places, we need to be real for a moment and face our baggage so we can let it go, even if it involves forgiveness. The Word says to bring all our cares to him, because he cares for us. We can trust God to replace our hurts with grace and love. It's so worth it.

Father, I invite the warmth of your love to pour into the cold parts of my heart. Help me to surrender these areas to you; even the deep buried hurts. Give me the grace to forgive. Amen (Read this prayer a few times, if you need to.)

Super Bloom

A flower blooming in the desert proves to the world that
adversity, no matter how great, can be overcome.
~ *Matshona Dhliwayo*

Isaiah 35:1
The desert and the parched land will be glad; the
wilderness will rejoice and blossom. Like the crocus,
it will burst into bloom; it will rejoice greatly
and shout for joy!

What an amazing sight it is to see the desert in super bloom. It only happens about every ten to fifteen years, so if you get to see the phenomenon, it's a rare and special sight. Imagine taking a walk through God's colorful garden of splendor in the desert sands. A place that you expect to be dry and dead is completely transformed and is now full of life and color. It's a picture of what he can do in our lives.

Today's scripture talks about a desert in super bloom, rejoicing greatly and shouting for joy! When was the last time you did that? We can all use more joy in our lives, right? If you haven't felt real joy lately, I speak that over you now. You can speak it over yourself by reading Isaiah 35:1 and applying it to yourself. You are the desert that will be glad. You will rejoice and blossom. You will burst into bloom and rejoice greatly! Are you feeling it yet? I challenge you to pray and speak this over yourself all day today (or longer), and see if you don't begin to feel real hope and joy creeping in. Make this one of your mantra verses that you go to - especially in the dark times - to remember that God is bringing your transformation. He's preparing your time to rejoice and shout for joy. Yes and amen!

Lord thank you for giving us the vision of transformation and joy coming to the dry desert places of our hearts. Help me to see it ahead, and begin to rejoice even before it arrives. Amen

Sea of Sand

The desert is so huge, and the horizon so distant, that they make a person feel small, and as if he should remain silent. ~ *Paulo Coelho*

Isaiah 41:10 NIV
Do not fear, for I am with you; do not be dismayed, for I am your God.

The desert is a place of extremes. It can be hot and dry during the day, and cold and desolate at night. It's a place where life seems scarce, and the landscape can seem barren and lifeless. But in the midst of this harsh environment, there is beauty to be found, and lessons to be learned about God's faithfulness.

In the Bible, we read about many desert experiences. The Israelites wandered in the desert for forty years, learning to trust in God's provision and guidance. Elijah fled to the desert, where he was fed by ravens and experienced God's presence in a still, small voice. And Jesus was led into the desert, where he was tempted by the devil, but ultimately relied on God's word to overcome.

The desert times of our life can be a place of spiritual growth, where we learn to trust God to provide and give us strength. It's a place where we can find a deeper faith, and where we can discover the value in the challenges we face. Believe this, and your battle is already won.

If you find yourself in a desert place, remember that God is with you. Someone once told me that we become what we focus on. If we focus on what we don't have, we live from a place of lack. But God has given us everything we need if we steward well what we do have. Today, bring your focus back to what God has already given you. If the vastness of your desert makes you feel small, just remember how big our God is.

My Jesus, thank you for being with me in the dry places. Please help me to rely on you more for strength and guidance. Teach me how to grow closer to you and be a good steward of what you have already given me. Amen

Sand Storms

The storms of life can make you better, or bitter.
~D.K. Olukoya

Habakkuk 1:9 NIV
Their hordes advance like a desert wind and
gather prisoners like sand.

A desert sand storm is a freak of nature. Named "Haboob" in the Sudan Arabian desert, it is a weather phenomenon that is a rather scary event.

I encountered a haboob in the Arizona desert some years ago as I was driving home from a road trip. I saw a wall of swirling sand ahead and pulled over immediately. What the heck? I'd never seen anything like it. Then I realized with sudden terror that it was coming toward me fast, and there was going to be no escape. I figured the only thing to do was to stay put and hope for the best. As the storm cloud engulfed me and my car, flying things were coming from out of no where, beating up my car… sticks, cactus, car parts! I was just hoping the wind wasn't strong enough to pick my car up and throw me around! After about twenty excruciating minutes and steady prayers, the storm passed. I was shook up, but also thrilled that I had just been through an extraordinary experience and lived to tell about it.

Life can throw us some curve balls, can't it? We can suddenly find ourselves in bad situations, with seemingly nothing we can do about it but pray. When there's no way out, we must go through, and praying for God's protection and guidance is the smartest thing we can do in these times. It's normal to feel a little fearful when things are out of our control, and it's not easy to push all that aside and trust God. But each time we do that, it gets easier. There is no scary thing on planet Earth that he doesn't know about. He will get us through it, and maybe even give us a story to tell others.

Has the Lord given you a story that someone else needs to hear to help them trust God in their situation?

Papa God, thank you for always being there for me to turn to in the scary times. Help me to trust you through every scary situation. Help me to learn the lessons and comfort others with the comfort you've given me. Amen

Week One: Journal

<u>Red Rocks:</u> Thank him for giving you beauty for ashes.

____

____

____

____

<u>Freezing Desert:</u> Giving God our hurts and forgiving.

____

____

____

____

<u>Super Bloom:</u> Thank God for the coming transformation.

____

____

____

____

____

Sea of Sand: Being thankful he is with you in the dry places.

____

____

____

____

Sand Storms: How has God gotten you through a storm?

____

____

____

____

Other Reflections:

____

____

____

____

Week Two

Desert Beauty

The desert tells a different story every time one ventures into it. ~ *Robert Edison Fulton Jr*

Isaiah 33:17 NIV
Your eyes will see the king in his beauty and
view a land that stretches afar.

The desert can be a challenging and harsh environment, with its intense heat, dryness, and rugged terrain, and yet life in the desert has learned to adapt and thrive in these hard conditions.

I have to say the desert fascinates me. When I was young and too busy to notice it, I would rush past the desert in an effort to just get through it on my travels. But if you stop and sit in the desert for a spell, you might be mesmerized by the simple beauty it offers. One of the things I love about it is that it's so empty and vast. No noise, no people, and the long views with nothing but wilderness. I enjoy the quietness of the desert. This is where I can really connect with our Father.

In many ways, the desert can be a metaphor for our own lives - full of challenges and adversity, but also full of potential and beauty. We will always have to deal with the challenges, but I try not to give it my full attention. Life can be full of beauty depending on what we focus on.

When I am in a dry spiritual place, I ask the Lord, "What do you want me to learn here?" I try to find quiet time to listen, but I don't always get answers. Many times the lessons aren't seen until further down the road. But we trust.

Getting close to nature is my favorite place to reflect on issues that are going on, and talk to Papa about it. Sometimes we might need to learn how to adapt, rather than hold out for that 'someday' when things will change or get back to normal. What if things will never get back to normal? What if this is the new normal? Can we look for the beauty here and now?

When it seems like life is too heavy, I purposefully look for beauty to redirect my focus. Could you use some time in nature to help you find the beauty in your day to day living?

Father, help me to find the beauty in every part of my life, especially in the challenges. Amen.

Desert Mountains

God moves mountains that we don't see.
~ *Guideposts Magazine*

1 Cor 13:2 NIV
...and if I have a faith that can move mountains,
but do not have love, I am nothing.

The desert is home to some of the most rugged and beautiful mountain ranges in the world. The desert mountains show us their layers and structure like no other mountains can. They look like solid rock, strong and immovable. Was God talking about spiritual things when he said our faith could move mountains?

I've had my share of mountains standing in the way of my progress. I remember a time when I was trying to buy my dream house, and everything seemed to be going along fine, until a past credit issue stopped everything in its tracks. It seemed like an immovable mountain, and I prayed passionately for God to move it for me. Finally, a new lender accepted my application and the deal went through. Thank you Lord! I know that I received my own little miracle that day.

If you're staring down a big mountain in your life, remember that God is like the solid rock mountain in the desert that we can turn to, and that he is still in the business of doing miracles. Our scripture today tells us that our faith in God's power can move our mountains. But don't forget the part about having love, or all those miracles mean nothing.

Maybe the whole point of this passage is to remind us to be loving toward others. How do we treat others in the middle of our obstacles? Are we serving others or just being self-serving in those times? Remember Solomon's prayer when God said he could have anything? He wanted wisdom to serve the people. Now there's an example of selfless love.

Thank you Lord, for the strong mountains that point to your power, and the lesson on how love means serving others. Amen

Coyotes

Coyote is always out there waiting, and coyote is always hungry. ~ *Navajo (Diné) proverb*

Ecclesiastes 9:4 NLT
There is hope only for the living. As they say, "It's better to be a live dog than a dead lion!"

There are valuable lessons to be learned from the coyotes of the desert. They live in a harsh and unforgiving place, but have adapted in their own unique way to the challenges of the arid landscape. These desert animals can teach us about perseverance, adaptability, and being survivors.

Sometimes we need all those things, don't we? I had a job in my twenties that really challenged me, with a boss that was unbelievably difficult. Some days I would lock my office door and just cry and pray for a way out. I wanted to walk out so many times, but my pastor had been teaching about having integrity, and I knew this was my test. So I bit my lip and persevered, while I started a new job search. After several interviews, I was confused about which job offer to take. My friend ask me, "If you could have any job you wanted, what would it be? Let's not limit God!" Long story short, my dream job was to work for myself, and God opened the doors for me to start my own business. He even used my old boss to endorse me and send me my first customer! What an awesome God we serve! I believe he honored me for taking the high road and doing the right thing.

That's how we act like the coyote - we do what we must to survive, with integrity. We do our part, and God does his part, and it all works together to bring us to a better place in the end.

I love You Lord, for teaching me the lessons that lead to blessings and rewards. Some lessons are hard, but I know they build character, and I'm so grateful you love me enough to make me more like you. Amen

Desert Night Sky

The desert, when the sun comes up. I couldn't tell where heaven stopped and the Earth began.
~ Tom Hanks

Song of Solomon 6:10
"Who is this, arising like the dawn, as fair as the moon, as bright as the sun, as majestic as an army with billowing banners?"

The desert is known for its wide-open spaces and rugged landscapes, but it is also home to some of the most stunning night skies on earth. When the sun sets and the stars come out, the desert sky displays the vastness of the universe like no where else. It's a place to marvel at His creation.

When I was in my twenties, I would drive out to the desert over a weekend just to spend the night under the stars. I remember a time when my younger sister and I drove out to the desert, about a hundred miles from our home town. We found a dirt road to drive down until we could get beyond any city lights or sounds of the freeway so we could see the night sky better. We took our sleeping bags and climbed out on the hood of my old '55 Oldsmobile, and lay back on the windshield to see how many shooting stars we could see. We could have stayed out there all night, but when we heard the coyotes start to howl, we decided to sleep in the car - windows up and the doors locked!

Looking out into the universe at night makes me feel very small and insignificant for sure. It's amazing to think about how small planet Earth really is in the grand scheme of things. And then we are only one person in eight billion people living here. Think about how special we are to be alive on this planet, when as far as we can see into the universe, we are the only place with life out there. Looking at the stars helps me to put my problems into perspective, and makes it easier to let things go that really aren't that important after all.

Thank you Father for showing us how big you really are by looking out into the universe. Help us to not take ourselves and our little problems so seriously. Amen

The Saguaro

Being negative only makes a difficult journey more difficult. You may be given a cactus, but you don't have to sit on it. *~Joyce Meyer*

2 Samuel 22:17-18 NIV
...thorns had come up everywhere, the ground was covered with weeds, and the stone wall was in ruins.

The Saguaro cactus is a protected species of cactus in Arizona. They transplant them when building roads in an effort to save them. I found them intriguing to look at. Each one different from the next.

The cactus may be looked upon by many in a negative way, because they are full of thorns and live in a hot, dry desert. But I've learned some interesting and positive facts about the Saguaro. In late Spring, they bloom pretty little white flowers on the tips of every arm. Later, the flowers die off and make sweet red fruit. Native Americans used to gather the fruit, and it has a wonderful sweet/tart flavor. The taste is like a cross between a kiwi and a strawberry.

I went on a Saguaro fruit gathering mission one year. I brought a fifteen foot long PVC stick with me to knock them off the top, but Saguaros are two to three times that tall! I had to find some growing on a hill and climb on rocks to get high enough to knock off a few fruit hoping I wouldn't fall into them. It was a prickly adventure, and I made some cactus apple fruit leather that my friends and family got to experience as Christmas gifts that year.

So what is the lesson here? There is always something positive to find in every ugly situation. We can take a clue from the quote and the scripture today. If we stay in that harsh negative place, thorns will come up and weeds start growing in our hearts. Eventually, our life is in ruins. There is power in positive thinking and looking for the good in things.

Father, help us to find the beauty and a positive thing about every thorny situation in our lives. Amen

Week Two: Journal

Desert Beauty: Finding the beauty in day to day living.

____

____

____

____

Desert Mountains: Moving mountains with Love.

____

____

____

____

The Coyotes: Surviving with integrity.

____

____

____

____

Desert Night Skies: How big is our God, and how small we are.

The Saguaro: A positive outlook to a thorny situation.

Other Reflections:

Week Three

ψψψ

Desert Sunset

Peace is seeing a sunset and knowing who to thank.
~Amish Proverb

Psalm 19:1 NIV
The heavens declare the glory of God; the skies
proclaim the work of his hands.

Sunsets are a stunning display of God's handiwork, and they seem especially colorful in the desert. Watching the colors of the sky slowly shift from gray and white, into pink and orange is one of my favorite things to do. It feels very peaceful, like the skies are bringing the issues of the day to a sweet end, leaving us with a bit of beauty to cap it off, and helping us to let go of any lingering heaviness.

Wouldn't it be wonderful if we could do that at the end of every day? What if we were to let go of any heaviness and just rest in another completed day? Can we be satisfied that we did the best we could, and let ourselves relax in knowing what ever we left undone, will be there for us tomorrow? I know from personal experience, that is not always what happens. I sometimes hold on to things into the night, and it keeps me awake. But the Word tells us, "Do not worry. Learn to pray about everything. Give thanks to God as you ask him for what you need." (Phil 4:6 NLT)

We can't always catch a sunset to help us let go of the day, but we can use the Philippians verse above as a prayer to give the concerns of each day to him so we can stop worrying, and end our day in a restful peace, knowing that what ever we left undone is in his hands. We might need to lean back into things in the morning, but for now, it's ok to let go. The ultimate bedtime prayer to end our days.

Papa God, thank you for always being there to take on our worries and concerns as we remember to pray about everything, and ask you for what we need. Amen

Balancing Rocks

This was rad to see! So many cool rocks! ~ *Unknown Traveler*

Song of Songs 8:5 NLT
Who is this coming up from the desert,
resting on her loved one?"

The photo today is from Marble Canyon - a place I visited a few times in Arizona. There are all these amazing balancing rocks scattered around the landscape that have you scratching your head wondering how they happened, and how they stay there without toppling over.

Our lives are sometimes a balancing act as we go through each day, aren't they? Our modern society packs more and more on our plates, and if we're honest, we may be guilty of overloading ourselves, because we want to do it all, and we say, "I've got this!" But then we find out it's not as easy as we thought, and it's created stress. We might need to take a thing or two off of our plates to create more margin in our lives.

I love this bit of scripture from Song of Songs today, that gives us a picture of a young girl coming up out of the desert with complete confidence in where she is at in this place and time in her life, because she is resting on her beloved . For us, that is the Lord.

If you feel like your life is out of balance, let this scripture give you a vision for something different. Picture yourself walking out of your desert with complete confidence as you rest in the Lord. If you need to take some action to create that margin, then give it some prayer and let go with confidence, knowing that you will be able to enter into that sweet rest with your Father.

Papa God, please keep pouring out your Spirit of wisdom on me to know what to keep and what to take off my plate to reduce stress and walk in your rest. Amen

Loneliest Road

Sometimes the road ahead is just a line to the horizon
that doesn't care if we run out of gas and reminds us
that we are tiny traveling blips in the vast macrocosm
of the universe. That's pretty much what it's like to
drive Highway 50 through Nevada.
~ *Article from TimeOut.com*

Psalms 62:1-2 NLT
My soul is quiet and waits for God alone. He is the One who
saves me. He alone is my rock and the One who saves me.
He is my strong place. I will not be shaken.

Sometimes the road we are on can feel pretty lonely, and seem to go on forever. There is a road in the desert going from California through Nevada that is called the 'loneliest road' because it stretches for miles and miles without a stop and no signs of human life. I've driven this and others like it myself, and after a while they can make one start to feel desperate to see some sign of life. The impending doom of getting stuck in a desert with no help in sight becomes real.

When we find ourselves in a spiritual and emotional place of loneliness, with seemingly no one to turn to, there is Psalm 62. This small passage in the Bible packs power. If you meditate on these words, it begins to sink into your spirit that you are not really alone. Papa God is there. He is our rock. He is the One that will save us. He is our strong place to run to. He is always guiding us and protecting us through this journey called "life".

Sometimes it's just the act of crying out to God that releases the anxiety and fears, and brings us relief. Letting the tears flow and absorbing the promises of his word will bring us to a better place. There is always an exchange in seeking God. When we give our hurts to him, we let those be replaced by his love, which gives us new hope and confidence to move forward from a better frame of mind.

Do you need to make an exchange with God today? His love for your hurts and fears?

Papa God, thank you for being there for me and offering me such a great exchange. Help me to make my offerings and receive your gifts and promises. Amen

Roadrunners

Roadrunner teaches how to find the hidden humor in situations all while showing you the path to greater productivity and efficiency. ~ *Roadrunner Symbolism*

Luke 13:19 NLT
It is like a mustard seed, which a man took and planted in his garden. It grew and became a tree, and the birds perched in its branches.

$\mathbf{E}$verything in God's creation has potential to be so much more than ordinary. Bugs aren't just bugs; butterflies have beauty that move us. Birds aren't just birds; they take flight and we marvel to watch them master the air. Creation was for God's pleasure, but I think he knew it would fill us with wonder.

The roadrunner is definitely a very unique bird to study, and I personally find joy when getting glimpses of them, which is a fairly rare occasion. It's interesting that we have a habit of assigning symbolism to animals that make them much more significant than just a simple creature. God gave us eyes in our hearts and souls that see beyond the ordinary.

In our modern society we can sometimes feel insignificant, but we need to remember that in all of the extraordinary elements of creation, we are actually his masterpiece. And even in our day to day routines, we can do extraordinary things. For example, the scripture today mentions the simple act of planting a seed. A seed planted in the ground may produce a tree that birds can call home. Planting a seed in someone's heart, can change their life forever. Just watch what happens when you find something extraordinary about a person in your day today, and tell them about how special they are. Plant a seed of joy, and ask the Lord to water it. I hope God continues to reveal what is special about you too!

Papa God, thank you for so much beauty and potential you display all around us. Help us to see the gifts you give each one of us that make us special and unique. May we shine a light on what makes others special too. Amen

Mesquite Trees

Leave it alone, mi amor. It's in the tree's
nature to be stubborn. It's a survivor."
~ Guadalupe Garcia McCall, *Under the Mesquite*

Jeremiah 17:7-8 (NIV)
But blessed is the one who trusts in the Lord, whose
confidence is in him. They will be like a tree planted by the
water that sends out its roots by the stream. It does not fear
when heat comes; its leaves are always green. It has no
worries in a year of drought and never fails to bear fruit.

The mesquite tree is a remarkable symbol of resilience, thriving in the hot and dry conditions of the desert. The mesquite tree's secret is that it draws its strength from deep roots that reach the moisture far beneath the earth.

Like the mesquite tree, we can draw strength and resilience from our faith and trust in God. With his help, we can endure the most difficult circumstances and come out stronger on the other side. This is why we must let our roots in the Lord grow deep and strong.

I think about how the strength of the mesquite tree not only helps itself, but provides resources to others as well. Its shade can save a life for anyone lost in the desert. The bean pods are edible, and the wood has a special fragrance and quality sought after for special purposes.

When we are strong in the Lord, it not only helps us in the hard times, but we become a beacon of hope for others. We can be the shelter they can rest in, and our lives become an example that shows there is still hope. There is always hope. Because of our strength and confidence, others can stand tall and strong. Is there someone you can offer strength to today?

Thank you Father for lessons we can learn from the tree that survives with its strong, deep roots. What a blessing to be able to use the strength you give me, to strengthen others. Help me to keep growing my roots deeper in you. Amen

Desert Sunsets: Ending our day in a restful peace.

Balancing Rocks: Walking out of our deserts with confidence.

Loneliest Road: Exchanging our hurts for his love..

Roadrunners: Finding extraordinary things about ourselves.

Mesquite Tree: Become strong to be a blessing to others.

Other Reflections:

Week Four

Palm Tree Oasis

Wild and free, just like a palm tree.
~ *laurewanders.com*

Psalm 92:12-14 NIV
The righteous flourish like the palm tree and grow like a cedar in Lebanon. They are planted in the house of the Lord; they flourish in the courts of our God. They still bear fruit in old age; they are ever full of sap and green.

The palm tree is a majestic and steadfast pillar in the desert, standing tall and unyielding in the harsh landscape. A true symbol of the desert oasis, these trees are like a life line of salvation. We know they are a sign that there will be water and relief from the sun.

The strength of the palm tree in the desert, is its ability to bend and not break, even in hurricane force winds. They can weather any storm, and survive the baking heat.

How can we dig into this kind of strength? Some days, we wonder, is it in us? Although we might not be able to handle real physical storms, our scripture today reminds us that we can flourish like the palm tree in our own worlds. Even in old age, we can expect to bear fruit and be full of life. Why? Because we are God's righteous people who have been planted in the house of the Lord! Our lives represent a desert oasis to the world, revealing the promises of God by our very existence. We hold out the hope of life to those who are lost. Our answer lies in serving others.

The world is a harsh place, and there are so many that need a refuge, even if they don't know what that looks like. What a difference we can make if we see ourselves as the palm tree of the Lord, planted to bring light and hope to others. Is there a thirsty soul you can show the way to the refreshing waters?

Papa God, I am amazed at how you see us and have set us apart to do a special work in the Earth. Help us to step into our role as your oasis in the desert. Amen

Cactus Flowers

The flower that blooms in adversity is the most beautiful of all. ~*Jooinn*

Song of Solomon 2:12 NLT
The flowers are springing up, the season of singing birds has come, and the cooing of turtledoves fills the air.

There is something special about cactus blooms. Maybe because of the environment they live in, their color and beauty seems to be magnified. Even in the bleakest conditions on planet Earth, life and beauty can be found.

Have you ever heard the saying, "We were born for such a time as this?" The thinking behind it, is that we were born into adversity, on purpose. As if what we have to offer was designed to fit exactly into what is needed most right now, in the time that we live in. The cactus blooms stick out in the desert landscape as something special to be noticed and appreciated. What if God put us into our landscape to stand out as something special?

Sometimes it's hard to see ourselves as 'special', and yet each of us are unique. A mentor recently told me that we need to be authentic and uniquely ourselves in this world. To do anything else (trying to be like someone else, or think that we aren't good enough because we aren't like others) is an insult to the God who made us. We have a place in this world, and a purpose to fulfill that no one other than us can do. That really freed me, because when I think about it, I've spent a lot of energy over the years trying to become what I thought was the 'status quo'.

This is not like the thinking some have about being different on purpose. How about we start being free to be who God made us to be, and honor that by being authentic?

Papa God, thank you for making me unique and special. I don't want to pretend to be someone I'm not. Help me to be authentically who you made me to be. Amen

Ancient Desert Fortress

King Herod's ancient fortress in Masada.

Matthew 2:7 NLT
*Then Herod called for a private meeting with the
wise men, and he learned from them the time
when the star first appeared.*

It is said that Herod built this fortress only a couple decades before the birth of Jesus, for protection. Then when the ancient Romans overtook Judea in the first century A.D., the grounds became a fortress for the Jewish people.

Was this the place where Herod heard about a Messiah being born, and talked to the wise men who were seeking the baby? He wanted to get intel so he could vanquish the rumor of a coming king. But history shows that Herod died before Jesus started his ministry, and his fortress didn't save him. In fact the Jewish people obtained the property after he was gone. How's that for poetic justice?

It's interesting to think about this landscape around Jesus' birth. Bethlehem is part of the Judean desert. It looks so inhospitable, and yet God was working out his plan of the ages there. Can anything good come out of the dry desert? That's a big YES. The miracle birth of Christ.

Are you in a desert that you feel nothing good can come out of? Maybe you need to think again. Is God working out the plan of your life while you wait in the desert? Is he thinking about your miracle? Something I learned recently, is that "things don't happen to us, they happen for us." If we look at our deserts like that, we begin to have anticipation for amazing things ahead. God is working all things together.

Father thank you for the places that bring scripture to life. Thank you for miracles in the desert. Thank you for my desert, and my miracle! Amen

Desert Waves

The Vermilion Cliffs National Monument has some of the most visually striking geologic sandstone.

Ezekiel 43:2 NLT
The sound of his coming was like the roar of rushing waters, and the whole landscape shone with his glory.

So much of the most phenomenal landscapes and geologic formations on planet Earth were clearly the direct result of a LOT of water (a global flood maybe?) rushing through and leaving its mark. Most scientists won't agree to that statement, and you may have another explanation, but what my eyes see, seem to line up with scripture. In an effort to minimize any spiritual accountability, the world strives to find another answer. I was once in that pool, but have since found that my faith doesn't need to have all the answers to simply believe.

In 1st Peter 1:17 we read, *"These trials will show that your faith is genuine. It is being tested as fire tests and purifies gold–though your faith is far more precious than mere gold."*

It's a hard fact, but our bible teaches that our faith will be tested, through our mistakes and through our trials. Someone recently said to me, "What if there are no mistakes? What if there are only lessons? And lessons may be taught again and again until they are learned." This reminds me that sometimes the lesson is to trust even if I don't have all the answers. We don't need to stress about figuring everything out. We may never understand why our spouse does certain things, or be able to change it. But we need to accept and love them anyway. We may never understand why we didn't get that promotion, but we need to serve the team leader well anyway. I may not sell a million books, but God wants me to write it anyway!

Our faith is far more precious than mere gold. We may not know the value of it until we pass over to be with our Lord, but it's enough for me to know I can trust the process. You can trust the process too.

Thank you Father for that inner peace to know it is well with my soul, and that I can trust you even though I don't have all the answers. Amen

Rare Beauty

Antique Arizona postcard with two
kinds of saguaro.

Luke 7:46
You neglected the courtesy of olive oil to anoint my head,
but she has anointed my feet with rare perfume.

Crested Saguaros have an unusual mutation resulting in the growth of large fan-shaped crests at the end of a saguaro's main stem and arms. Something went wrong with the DNA of the cactus while it was growing, and it got a little creative! Scientists have tried to pin down what causes this recurring phenomenon, but so far have not been able to. I wonder if it's a long lost strain of cactus that occasionally shows itself. Either way, it's a rare and beautiful scene. It's estimated to only occur once out of every 200,000 cactus.

Rare things always peak our interest, especially if they are a real anomaly. I think we love to experience something new that we've never encountered before. Also, rare things have more value.

They say that it may take a Saguaro cactus about seventy five years before it grows its first arm. They grow very slowly, only about one and a half inches in it's first eight years! So the crested saguaro might be hundreds of years old before they bloom.

Some of us make the mistake of thinking we are too old to make a difference or add any beauty to the world. Not true! We might not have as much energy as we did when we were younger, but we have so much learned wisdom to offer the world. I plan on being a rare bird and blossom in my latter years. How about you? It's never too late, my friend.

Papa God, thank you for glimpses of rare beauty to inspire and encourage us to give away what you have given us to a world that needs your wisdom; something that is becoming more and more rare to find. Amen

Week Four: Journal

Palm Tree Oasis: How can we be an oasis to a thirsty world?

____

____

____

____

Cactus Flowers: Being authentically who God made me to be..

____

____

____

____

Ancient Fortresses: Thanking God for our desert miracle.

____

____

____

____

Desert Waves: Trust. We don't have to understand everything.

____

____

____

____

Rare Beauty: How can we blossom in rare and beautiful ways?

____

____

____

____

____

Other Reflections:

____

____

____

____

____

Week Five

Slot Canyons

Water paths sculpted the red rocks into a piece of art.

Psalm 119:35 TPT
Guide me on the paths that please you.

Antelope Canyon in the Arizona desert is a long and twisty slot canyon. As you walk through, the path gets skinnier, until at one point it's a real squeeze to get through. These tight canyons were made by flash floods that came through cracks in the rocks with a bit of force. This canyon still gets flooded during a monsoon season, so the water and sands are still carving and smoothing the canyon walls. The Native Americans who own the land, won't allow anyone to visit the canyon when rain threatens for this reason. It can be a dangerous path.

As believers, we walk a different path than the world. The world doesn't understand why we follow a God they can't see, or how we can trust, when sometimes, our paths lead us into hard times. Yes, desert seasons are not easy for anyone, but have you considered that it may be required sometimes to get us back on the right path?

Personally, there have been times I've felt like I've been in a 'rut' or otherwise stuck without knowing what path to take. When we ask our Father to guide us on the paths that please him, we can't go wrong. It may not be an instant fix, but I believe he begins working things together to show us a better way. When we can speak the Word over our issues, it can't come back to him without accomplishing what he sent it out to do. (See Isaiah 55:11)

The truth is, our Father gives us the power to make our own choices in life, and we can certainly get ourselves into trouble - what parent couldn't say that about their child? But thank God for this verse! We can ask him to redirect our steps toward the path that pleases him. This is the first step in the right direction.

Papa God, thank you for being there to turn to when we find ourselves on the wrong path. Thank you for helping us adjust our sails to return to paths that please you. Amen

Death Valley

We drove through the Mojave Desert, Owens Valley and Death Valley, and the dust entered our bloodstream and flowed through to every part of our body. ~Karl Wiggins

Deut 32:9 NLT
He found them in a desert land, in an empty, howling wasteland. He surrounded them and watched over them; he guarded them as he would guard his own eyes.

I recently took a trip to visit Death Valley and spent a few days there to get some inspiration for this book. As God would have it, I was experiencing my own little 'desert trial' at the time. So when I asked him what lessons he would teach us in the deepest, driest, hottest desert, I was all ears.

One of the things Holy Spirit showed me there, was that the physical desert can kill us if we stay too long, and we aren't prepared, or if we don't do something to get ourselves out. Too long in a spiritual desert, can break our spirits too.

I was reminded that when we are talking about desert seasons, sometimes these dead zones want to draw us into depression, and we can get stuck. I think what the Spirit was saying, is "don't give up." Maybe a better way to say it is, "don't give in to it." Fight it every time! But if you are in a time of depression, don't stay there. Fight your way out. Remember that Jesus died for your freedom!

I believe we have these trials so that when harder things come, we won't be shaken. Paul says that no discipline is easy when we are going through it, but in the end we are stronger. Paul even said that it was a great honor for him to go through tests and trials, because the Lord deemed him worthy to be tested and used that way. Did we sign up for this? Yes, when we surrendered our lives to God, we asked him to come in. He's never going to leave us the same, and will be making us more like Jesus every day.

Our scripture today tells the story of God watching over his people in the desert and guarding them. Notice that he didn't take them out of the desert, but he helped them get through it. He hasn't gone anywhere. He's there to help us get through our deserts too.

Lord, help me to trust you to get me through my deserts, and to be looking for the lessons to be learned. Amen

Bare Mountains

The hardest mountain to climb is the one within.
J. Lynn

1 Cor 14:25 NIV
...as the secrets of their hearts are laid bare. So they
will fall down and worship God, exclaiming,
"God is really among you!"

In the depths of Death Valley you can't help noticing that the mountains are completely naked and bare, with all their layers and scars out in the open to plainly see. Nothing hidden.

When I was visiting the area, I took time to sit in the heat and study the bare mountains. The thought came to mind about how being vulnerable and exposed - like these mountains - is a place where we can meet honestly with God. With nothing in the way, we can bare the secrets of our heart to him purely and wholly. When we become this open with the Lord, his presence is so near, we can do nothing else but fall down in worship, just as today's scripture explains. Can you imagine how cleansing that could be?

We can all be 'pretenders' sometimes, hiding our hurts so well, until we know that something needs to give or we are going to break down. Thank God we can come to him and surrender those feelings for relief and help. When you do, waste no time in baring your scars and layers for him to see and heal. Come into his presence with singing, and tears. His love and grace is waiting.

Take a moment to present your heart and feel his presence.

Jehovah God, my Healer, I leave nothing hidden before you. I ask you to heal this heart. I take these secrets and leave them in the death valley of your love, and in exchange I present my worship. My pure, honest worship, with thanksgiving. Amen

Big Horn Sheep

The desert bighorn ranges through the dry, desert mountains of eastern CA, much of NV, northwest AZ, and southern Utah.

Leviticus 22:23 NIV
You may, however, present as a freewill offering an ox or a sheep.

One of the more amazing views in the southwest is the Painted Desert area in Arizona. It becomes even more special when you get to see the big horn sheep lounging around on the colorful hills.

Sheep make me think about the offerings in the old testament, where the Israelites were required to give animals to atone for their sins, and to honor the Lord in many ways. There was one offering called the "freewill" offering. This is a beautiful concept, because it's not about making a sacrifice out of duty, but just because you love and respect the Creator. Just look at everything he's given us! He deserves our sacrifice of worship, and the painted desert seems to be showing us how to do just that. This desolate place doesn't have much to offer; with no shade, no grass, and nothing to harvest, but the many colors and dimensions of the hills are what the desert brings before the Almighty. And, it's stunning.

When we are in our desert places, we may not feel like we have anything to offer in worship, and that's when the freewill offering comes into play. We worship him just because of who he is. Just because we love him. And don't be surprised if this type of worship becomes the deepest, most spirit filled time of your life. It's in the desert places that we dig deep, through all the pain, to reach for the love. The worship itself pushes the pain away, and brings us right into his presence, and we find healing.

My precious Father, I give you my freewill offering, even in the hard desert places. You are worthy. Amen

Desert Monuments

Monuments are the grappling irons that binds one
generation to another. ~Joseph Joubert

1 Chronicles 18:3 NIV
David defeated Hadadezer king of Zobah, in the
vicinity of Hamath, when he went to set up
his monument at the Euphrates River.

Monuments in the old testament are mentioned in many
different ways. Today's passage mentions how monuments
were setup when a King won a battle, to mark the new

territory. I think it's a noble idea. What if we setup monuments when we've won a battle (spiritual or otherwise), proclaiming that we now own this space? "See my monument marker? Come no further!" Those defeated enemies are warned that we have conquered, and have no intention of giving back any of the newly acquired territory. Like drawing a line in the sand.

In the southwest, the monuments in the desert are phenomenal. Check out Monument Valley or Arches National Park. These amazing formations stand on the desert floor as a memorial or monument to the past. What are we supposed to remember from the past here? A flood came through and left these monuments in a strangely artistic form, reminding us of a past E. L. E. (Extinction Level Event).

The story of Joshua shares how God told him to be strong and courageous, that the Lord was with him and would help him defeat the enemy he was facing. The people's faith was tested when they were asked to step into the water to cross the Jordan River, and when they acted on their faith, dry land appeared and they walked safely across. Twelve of the strong soldiers picked up rocks in the middle of the river bed as they were going across, and then made a monument on the other side to remember this event. The Lord had delivered them.

In the same way, we can setup monuments that represent victories hard won, and stake our claim that the enemy has been defeated. Whether you setup stones, or simply write it down in a journal, the act of claiming your victory solidifies it. What victory are you claiming today?

Father, thank you for the victories. Help me to be strong and courageous, to claim my win and make my monuments. Amen

<u>Slot Canyons:</u> *Asking for guidance for the right path to take.*

____

____

____

____

<u>Death Valley:</u> *Don't stay in depression. Find a way out.*

____

____

____

____

<u>Bare Mountains:</u> *Bare your heart completely to the Lord.*

____

____

____

____

<u>Slot Canyons:</u> *Asking for guidance for the right path to take.*

____

<u>Big Horn Sheep:</u> *Make a freewill offering in your desert place.*

____

____

____

____

<u>Desert Monuments:</u> *What victories are you claiming today?*

____

____

____

____

____

<u>Other Reflections:</u>

____

____

____

____

____

Week Six

The Outback

The mysterious vast single stone, that lies at
Australia's heart. Ayer's Rock. Also known as Uluru.

1 Samual 2:2 NIV
There is no one holy like the Lord; there is no one besides
you; there is no Rock like our God.

Visiting Australia has always been on my bucket list. The
desert in Australia is quite different than any where else, with
its brightly colored sand, and the famous and mysterious red
rock sitting in the outback desert.

Ayers Rock is situated in a huge flat desert area, so it stands out as an anomaly and can be seen from a long way off. It's like a beacon for any person or animal lost in the great outback.

Jesus is that rock we look for to find shelter and safety when we feel lost. The more we walk with God, the more we will be looking for him as our relief from life's storms. How will Jesus calm our storms, you ask? By seeking his peace, we let go of the anxieties we are holding on to. We can't hold on to faith and fear at the same time.

Here's what it looks like for me. I start with prayer, and sometimes a few tears. I open my heart to him, and earnestly seek him with my words and maybe some worship too. Songs that have meaning to us, help us to sing spirit to spirit, our spirit to the Holy Spirit. That's when the release comes and those proverbial chains are broken. You feel lighter and something inside has shifted. I'm not saying the problem or issue is instantly solved, although that can sometimes happen. But you know in your heart that God has heard, and somehow he is carrying part of the load. You know he is working things out, and that you are not alone. We may need to repeat this process to get our breakthrough, but it will come.

Today, if there is something that you feel lost about, look for the rock in the desert. Jesus, standing like a beacon offering shelter and relief from your storm. Reach out for it. Sing him a song. Thank him for working things out for you. Find a scripture to stand on, and speak it out over your situation. You'll feel the fear leaving, and your faith growing.

Papa God, help me to look for you in the desert places, like a beacon calling me home. Amen

Bloom Anyway

Water is a deserts' gold. ~ Matshona Dhliwayo

Psalm 63:1
You, God, are my God, earnestly I seek you;
I thirst for you, my whole being longs for you, in a
dry and parched land where there is no water.

There are times when life feels so cracked and dry, it doesn't seem like you can eek out any joy at all. I know the feeling, and I say, bloom anyway! I love this photo that shows the bright blossoms growing through the cracks in the dead, dry desert. Just add a little water, and look what happens. The desert blooms in spite of itself!

What if you let the Holy Spirit pour out the oil of joy on you? What if you gave yourself to fully worship in spirit and truth? What if you rejoiced anyway? But how? How do you do that when your voice is like dry bones? You dig. Deep.

If you don't know how to dig that deep, let me suggest you spend some time in the Psalms. You'll find some songs of David where he is crying his heart out. He digs deep and makes a song to the Lord out of his grief. Let David give you inspiration. You'll notice that so many times he will be crying out to God in agony, but then whispers that he knows God hasn't forsaken him. He knows God is his source, his strength and his deliverer.

When those dry dead times come, dig into the Word and take a deep drink of water from the fountain of God. *"For with you is the fountain of life; in your light we see light."* (Psalm 36:9) Share your light with someone today, and you will sense the oil of joy pouring out. Joy is coming!

Pour out your oil on me Lord. Let me stand under the fountain of life that can only come from you. Let me see your light again Lord. I love you, and I will bloom anyway! Amen.

Desert Cat

The bobcat has adapted to survive in marginal habitats.
~ Arizona-Sonora Desert Museum

Job 39:21-22 NIV
It paws fiercely, rejoicing in its strength,
and charges into the fray.
It laughs at fear, afraid of nothing.

Have you ever spied a bobcat in the wild? Not many of us have. (My friend Wayne got very lucky with this shot.) They are very stealthy animals, and although cats are not mentioned specifically in the Bible, other animals are portrayed with some of the same traits these cats have - fierce, strong, and afraid of nothing.

The bobcat has survived in the harsh desert environments, because they have learned to adapt. That means they find a way, and don't give up. Sometimes we have to press in and find a way too, so we don't give up when life gets hard. So here's another bit of encouragement, because I've been there, and I know; a little encouragement goes a long way.

I've always been a strongly determined person that pushes through things to find a way to get to the other side, but I know that not everyone is like that. It might have been my tough up-bringing that made me a bit fierce, and I'm thankful for that, even though it was hard and I have a few regrets. But regrets don't have to keep us down. What could have been doesn't matter. It's what you do with what you're given that counts.

Please remember, that every moment in your life has made you who you are today, and if it makes you into a fierce, strong person who laughs at fear, then hallelujah! You are God's beautiful and prized masterpiece.

Thank you Father for every moment - even the hard ones - that make me who I am, your uniquely loved child. Amen.

Deep Canyons

As you go through life, you've got to see
the valleys as well as the peaks.
~Neil Young

Psalm 115:16 NIV
The highest heavens belong to the Lord,
but the earth he has given to mankind.

Paria canyon in the northern AZ desert, is an amazing water way through an incredibly deep canyon. The walls stretch up to eight hundred feet high, and that can make one feel like a tiny ant in the landscape, powerless in the face of Earth's elements, ready to be squashed by the next flow of water coming around the bend.

On the other hand, these places can also bring out a childlike wonder and awe in knowing that all this was given to mankind to steward by an Almighty Creator. Earth belongs to us! A gift from our Father. This perspective changes everything.

In our spiritual desert places, we can get absorbed in the negative possibilities, and not always see what a gift we've been given. Every trial represents an opportunity for growth and elevating our lives. *"Dear brothers and sisters, when troubles of any kind come your way, consider it an opportunity for great joy. For you know that when your faith is tested, your endurance has a chance to grow.." James 1:2-3 NLT*

I know it's not natural for us to feel joy in the middle of trials, but I think we can move toward that experience over time. What if we made a conscious effort to pause and start looking for the joy, asking, "What is the lesson here?", and smile. Can we dare to imagine what it might look like to actually have joy about a trial we are going through? When the deep walls of our trials are closing in around us, what if we look up, smile and say, "Thank you for this gift." Ha HA!!

Lord, help me to remember that your joy is my strength in every situation. Amen

Desert River

Politicians wanted to mine the Grand Canyon for
zinc and copper, and Theodore Roosevelt said, "No."
~David Brinkley

1st Peter 1:7 NLT
*These trials will show that your faith is genuine. It is being
tested as fire tests and purifies gold—though your faith is
far more precious than mere gold. So when your faith
remains strong through many trials, it will bring you
much praise and glory and honor on the day when Jesus
Christ is revealed to the whole world.*

The Colorado River runs for 1,450 miles, starting in Colorado, and then winding its way through hot, dry deserts in Utah, Arizona and California. A famous part of the river passes through the majestic Grand Canyon, a marvel to see. This ancient waterway and the canyon hold knowledge about our planet that only those with eyes to see can capture, although its secrets are there for all to see if they would.

Sometimes that's how it is with our own trials. Hard times can feel like a long twisty road through our lives, leaving scars and deep hurts. And yet they also hold secrets we can learn, if our hearts are willing.

Have you ever heard the saying, "No pain, no gain"? I sometimes think that's how these things work. Think about the pain that Jesus went through to save us. What about the pain all the apostles and Paul went through to birth the church. We are not exempt. We are in the company of noble men and women of the Bible that all went through many trials. How about we turn our cheek and pull ourselves up by the boot straps and join the fight? We have our part to play in Gods' plan. The secret to learn here is that we are bigger and more important to the plan that we may realize.

Today's scripture gives us another glimpse of how precious and valuable these trials really are in preparing us for the future, the day of Jesus' return, and eternity. Our reward is coming, so we need to work through these trials and get every last lesson , grow in our faith, and stay on track.

Lord, I'm standing strong to do my part, and I want to learn the lessons you have for me to develop my faith and prepare for eternity with you! Amen? Amen. Amen!

Week Six: Journal

The Outback: *How is Jesus your rock.*

____

____

____

____

Bloom Anyway: *Digging deep to rejoice in hard times..*

____

____

____

____

Desert Cat: *Learning to adapt when life gets hard.*

____

____

____

____

Deep Canyons: Opportunities in our trials

____

____

____

____

Desert Rivers: Learning lessons and staying on track.

____

____

____

____

Other Reflections:

____

____

____

____

Meet My Jesus

He died for you. (Yes, you.)

Romans 10:9 NIV
If you declare with your mouth, "Jesus is Lord,"
and believe in your heart that God raised him
from the dead you will be saved.

Maybe you already know my Jesus, but I could not close this book without giving you the invitation to receive him into your heart, in case you've never taken that step.

Not sure? Then **let's make sure** you don't go another minute without knowing without a doubt that he knows you and loves you. That he actually died so that you could come into his household and become an adopted son or daughter of the Most High God. Come without hesitation into the life he has for you. A life full of freedom and peace deep in your soul, because you *know* you are accepted just the way you are. Believe, and receive the gift of the Holy Spirit placed in the middle of your heart to intimately know without a doubt *who's* you are.

The story of Jesus is well known - I'm sure you've heard it before. Father God sent his one and only son to be the ultimate sacrifice for us. He paid the price for sin in the world, so we don't have to. It was a horrible death, but then a miracle happened. He awoke from death and was the first to go to be with the Father. But his sacrifice made it possible for anyone who would believe to join him. Not just in heaven, but on a spiritual journey here and now, to grow into the best version of ourselves - and maybe bring a few folks along with us.

It's this easy: If you believe in your heart, tell him directly: "Jesus, I believe you died for me! I believe you were raised from the dead. I ask you to breath the gift of the Holy Spirit on me so I can know you deep in my soul." Now tell someone! Find your tribe of other believers and get connected to a local church. Congratulations on beginning your spiritual journey! Welcome to the Family!

If you said that prayer for the first time, would you send me a note to tell me you met my Jesus?
https://www.cedarridgebooks.com/contact-us

Photo credits:

Cover — Nate Hovee
Introduction — Jenifoto
Red Rocks — Heber Lopez
Frozen Desert — Jenny Hernandez
Super Bloom — Ron Thomas
Sea of Sand — Lucyna Koch
Sand Storms — AZ Dept of Public Safety
Desert Beauty — Nate Hovee
Desert Mountains — Jack Brauer
Coyotes — Sylvain Cordier
Desert Night Sky — David Arment
The Saguaro — Dulcey Lima on Unsplash
Desert Sunset — wallpapers.com
Balancing Rock — Wayne Schwetje
Loneliest Road — travel-lingual.com
Road Runners — Ann Newman
Mesquite Trees — Eutoch
Palm Tree Oasis — Benedek
Cactus Flowers — visitcalifornia.com
Ancient Desert Fortress — Mindaugas Dulinskas
Desert Waves — Mike Jones
Rare Beauty — 1930-1945 Vintage Postcard
Slot Canyons — Private Collection
Death Valley — Private Collection
Bare Mountains — Private Collection
Big Horn Sheep — Kevin Griffith
The Outback — Meg Jerrard
Bloom Anyway — @ienjoyhiking
Desert Cat — Wayne Schwetje
Deep Canyon — Courtesy Bryce Cyn Natl Park
Desert River — Christin Healy
Meet My Jesus — wallpapers.com

If you enjoyed this book,

Please leave me a review on one or all of

these online bookstores:

www.Amazon.com

www.BarnesAndNoble.com

www.BooksAMillion.com

THANK YOU!

DEVOTIONS
From the Earth
Mountains

Inspiring devotions from nature with a theme about creations' beauty in the mountains.

DEVOTIONS
From the Earth
Skies

Inspiring devotions from nature with a theme about the vast skies and God's Word.

DEVOTIONS
From the Earth
Waters

Inspiring devotions from nature with a theme about the healing waters on the Earth.

About the Author

Linda Carter is a wife and mother of one, a grandmother of six, and a lover of Jesus. She has been an entrepreneur for thirty three years as a work-from-home mom, while nurturing her gifts as an author and bible teacher along the way. Her captivating teachings and writing springs from a life time of walking with God, and her connection with the natural world as a certified California Naturalist. She enjoys learning how to be a better steward of this amazing creation we have been given. Linda sees God's beautiful design in every created thing, with an eye to find the spiritual lessons contained in them.

With years of experience being involved with church ministry, mentoring and outreach, Linda has become a beacon of inspiration for those seeking spiritual growth and empowerment. She also loves teaching others how to appreciate and care for our beautiful planet. Her love for the natural world has played a pivotal role in shaping her unique views on life and spirituality. She shares her insights and wisdom from a fresh perspective, bringing nature's peace into her writings.

Whether she's found in the pages of her written works, mentoring others through the intricacies of scripture, or exploring the great outdoors, Linda Carter inspires us to step out in our faith, gain knowledge, and develop a deep appreciation for the beauty that surrounds us. She continues to inspire individuals on their spiritual journeys.